W9-AZA-548

How
UNDERWEAR
Got Under There

A BRIEF HISTORY

One of the most humorous examples of underwear paranoia occurred in the 1990s with the introduction of the Teacher Barbie doll. There was a huge outcry from concerned adults that the doll wasn't wearing underpants! Never mind that many Barbie dolls were sold without underwear . . . this one was a TEACHER, they said, and she ought to be dressed appropriately. The furor became so intense that the manufacturer actually recalled the doll and reissued it with underwear! The no-panty version became a valuable collectors' item.

About 60-70% of American men prefer snug briefs to loose boxers.

"Discussion of underwear and toilet articles, and their merit or their use, is unpleasant in polite conversation."
—Emily Post,
The Fundamentals of Good Behavior

The town of Inishmaan in Ireland is one of the few areas where boys as well as girls were known to wear woolen petticoats. It was believed that these garments not only kept them warm, but confused evil spirits who came to kidnap little boys.

Did you ever wonder why we're so embarrassed to be seen in our underwear when our bathing suits usually cover even less of our bodies?

Why do you think a pullover-style undershirt was called a "bachelor's shirt" in the nineteenth century? It was assumed that an unmarried man needed a garment without buttons, because if one fell off, he wouldn't be capable of sewing it back on himself!

Inuit girls living around the turn of the twentieth century sometimes wore reindeer skin leggings beneath their dresses. The hair of the deer faced inside, which helped retain heat.

Ever notice that the women in old movies and books always seem to faint when they get upset? Turns out that women wearing corsets passed out because their organs were so constricted by their corsets that they could not function properly.

OTHER PUFFIN NONFICTION BOOKS
YOU MAY ENJOY

How UNDERWEAR Got Under There

A BRIEF HISTORY

KATHY SHASKAN
ILLUSTRATED BY REGAN DUNNICK

PUFFIN BOOKS
An Imprint of Penguin Group (USA)

PUFFIN BOOKS
Published by the Penguin Group
Penguin Group (USA) LLC
375 Hudson Street
New York, New York 10014

USA * Canada * UK * Ireland * Australia
New Zealand * India * South Africa * China

penguin.com

A Penguin Random House Company

First published in the United States of America by Dutton Children's Books,
a division of Penguin Young Readers Group, 2007
Published by Puffin Books, an imprint of Penguin Young Readers Group, 2015

Text copyright © 2007 by Kathy Shaskan
Illustrations copyright © 2007 by Regan Dunnick

Image credits:
Pages 15, 17, 36, 37, 50, 52: Warshaw Collection of Business Americana–
Underwear, Archives Center, National Museum of American History.
Behring Center, Smithsonian Institution.

Page 23: Warshaw Collection of Business Americana–Ladies Clothing, Archives Center,
National Museum of American History. Behring Center, Smithsonian Institution.

Pages 30, 34 (bottom), 42: Warshaw Collection of Business Americana–Corsets, Archives Center,
National Museum of American History. Behring Center, Smithsonian Institution.

Penguin supports copyright. Copyright fuels creativity, encourages diverse voices,
promotes free speech, and creates a vibrant culture. Thank you for buying an authorized
edition of this book and for complying with copyright laws by not reproducing, scanning,
or distributing any part of it in any form without permission. You are supporting
writers and allowing Penguin to continue to publish books for every reader.

THE LIBRARY OF CONGRESS HAS CATALOGED THE DUTTON EDITION AS FOLLOWS:
Shaskan, Kathy.
How underwear got under there : a brief history / Kathy Shaskan ; illustrated by Regan Dunnick.
pages cm.
Summary: A humorous look at the science, fashion, and social ramifications of underwear throughout history.
ISBN: 978-0-525-47178-3 (hardcover)
[1. Underwear—Juvenile literature. 2. Fashion—History—Juvenile literature.]
I. Dunnick, Regan, ill. II. Title.
TT670 .S53 2007
2009278514

Puffin Books ISBN 978-0-14-751448-6

Printed in the United States of America

1 3 5 7 9 10 8 6 4 2

To Paul and Noël, who make the journey fun
—K. S.

To Debbie, Brandon, Jean, Perry, Joyce, Ed,
and my good friend Stretch
—R. D.

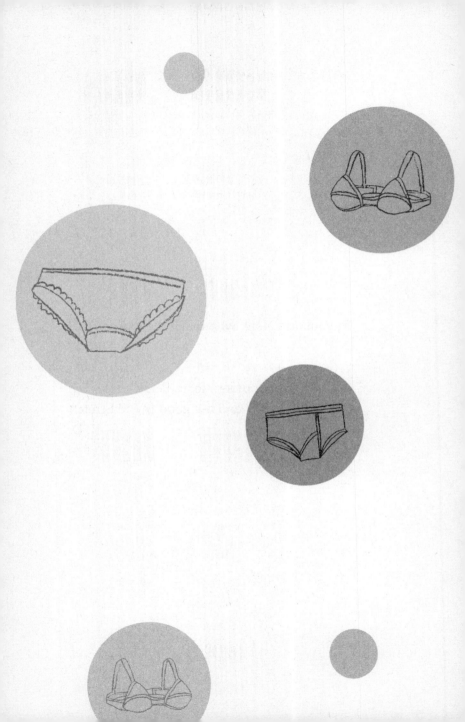

CONTENTS

How
UNDERWEAR
Got Under There

A BRIEF HISTORY

A "BRIEF" INTRODUCTION

Our poor underclothes! They can't seem to get any respect. We make jokes about them and stuff them in the backs of our dresser drawers. We're embarrassed to be seen in them. We're even embarrassed to be seen near them.

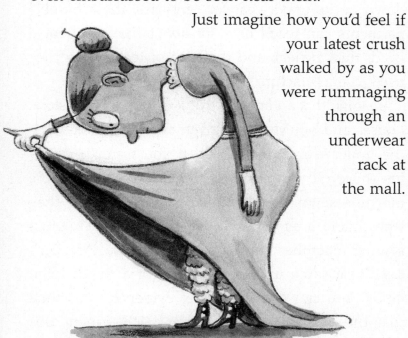

Just imagine how you'd feel if your latest crush walked by as you were rummaging through an underwear rack at the mall.

Though we trust these garments to be closest to our skin, shielding and protecting the most tender and private areas of our bodies, some of us blush at the mere mention of underwear. (Can you picture reading aloud in class and seeing the word *underpants* or *thong* coming up in the next sentence? Sheer torture!) Centuries ago, people whispered about their "unmentionables" when they absolutely had to talk about their underwear.

Even though the human race has been looking down on its underwear for centuries, these humble garments can teach us a lot about the way people lived, their beliefs, and the type of technology they used to manufacture their clothing.

Imagine that an antique trunk is found in a historic house, and you've been given the job of studying the underwear found inside. If you were to examine those old-time undies and find that they were machine-sewn, you'd immediately know that they were made after 1850. Why? Because that's when sewing machines came into general use. And let's say those same undies are made of a rough linen fabric. You can use that bit of evidence to assume that the original owners weren't rich. Linen rubs

Before the mid-1800s, there
was no such thing as sizes in
underwear. Clothing was hand-sewn
and custom-fitted for a
particular person.

uncomfortably against the skin, so most rich people preferred softer, more expensive materials like silk.

Even historians who study clothing have to work hard to "uncover" information about underwear. Consider this: When someone in your family preserves an item of clothing for future generations, or has a photo taken in a unique outfit, or writes about clothing in a diary, it is usually some special *outer* garment—a prom dress, a wedding tuxedo, a graduation gown. Hardly anybody saves or writes about their own underwear.

The same held true for our ancestors. We know what they wore to coronations, weddings, inaugurations, and balls, because they mentioned these special outfits in their letters and memoirs. Some people even had their portraits painted in them. They didn't bother to write about their underclothes because they just didn't think they were important.

But what we *do* know about our ancestors' underclothes is fascinating. So let's take a peek beneath the skirts of history.

The only images we have from the days before the invention of photography are drawings and paintings. When people took the time to sit for portraits, they wore their best clothes. That's why underwear and everyday clothing are harder to document.

PROTECTION

Modern underpants are the descendants of a funny little garment called the loincloth. You've seen it—it's that weird diaper-like thing that Tarzan wears as he swings through the jungle.

The loincloth has a very interesting history. People from all over the world who never met and never had the chance to compare fashion notes all came up with very similar types of loincloths.

At first glance that might seem amazing, but really, it makes perfect sense. If you lived back then, how many times would you need to walk naked past a patch of sticker bushes or cacti before you decided that it might be a good idea to grab some fabric and wrap it around your bottom? Most ancient people managed to figure that out, too.

Some early people tied simple pieces of cloth or animal skins around their waists, skirt-style, and left it at that. Others (perhaps the ones who had to walk through tall, sharp grasses) decided that their private parts could use a bit more protection. They started tucking pieces of the material through their legs as well.

But the original loincloths weren't underwear. They were only-wear. Later, as people began to layer their clothing, the loincloth and its descendants became the garment closest to the skin.

The loincloth is just one example of how underwear has been used as protection for the body. Another protective undergarment from the past is the gambeson. It was a long jacket-style undergarment that was worn by knights under their suits of armor. Thick, puckery, and stuffed with fiber or horsehair, the gambeson felt something like the quilted bed-spreads we use today. It prevented the sharp edges of the armor from rubbing against the skin. But that wasn't its only job. The gambeson was also meant to cushion the knight from the blow of an enemy weapon. The armor couldn't do that, because its hard surface was designed mainly to keep the weapon from piercing the skin.

Mongolian warriors serving under Genghis Khan in the thirteenth century also knew the value of protective underwear. Since the bow and arrow were their primary weapons, they became experts in removing arrows from the body. They designed densely woven silk under-shirts that arrows could not tear easily. The fabric was then grasped and twisted to help remove the arrow.

When the Disney film *Tarzan* opened in Israel, some religious groups objected to the advertising posters that went up around the city. Calling the depiction of Tarzan in a loincloth offensive, they demanded their removal. Disney refused, and the movie went on to become a big hit.

Have you ever gotten hit with a baseball or a

Most American men choose briefs over boxers.

hockey puck in one of your . . . um, *sensitive* areas? Then you know why protective underwear is so important in sports—and there are more types than you'd ever imagine.

In order to learn to spin and jump, figure skaters practice constantly and keep falling down until they get it right. So they need special undergarments with extra padding on the thighs and rear. Female fencers wear one-piece molded plastic chest guards tucked into their jackets. Men wear protective cups over their genitals in many different sports.

*Protective undergarments are a necessity in the sports world:
a hockey player's athletic cup takes the sting out of a
fast-moving puck; chest protectors shield female fencers;
fireproof underwear can save a race-car driver from a
fiery death; padded underwear protects cyclists.*

Professional cyclists develop "saddle sores" on their rears if they don't wear cushioned shorts or underpants. (How sore do you think your "saddle" would be if you rode the 2,300-mile Tour de France bicycle race without some kind of padding?)

Sometimes protective garments are job related. Firefighters, race-car drivers, and others who need to shield their skin from burns can wear flame-retardant undershirts and pants. People who work around dangerous chemicals can wear underwear that protects their skin from accidental spills. Business travelers in dangerous parts of the world sometimes choose to wear bulletproof underwear beneath their clothing.

Sometimes people wear special undergarments in search of a different otherworldly type of protection. Some might call it superstition, but the idea of sacred undergarments goes back at least as far as the ancient Babylonians. Often these garments had fringe, which has a long history as a symbol of God's protection.

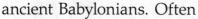

"King Tut" is the nickname we use for Tutankhamen, Egypt's famous Boy King, who ruled from age nine until his death at about eighteen. Many lovely linen garments were buried with the young king: tunics, shirts, gloves, socks, and 145 underpants! In recent years, textile experts around the world have been making reproductions of King Tut's clothing so that we can see them in their original colors. At first they wanted to dye the fabrics in the same way as the ancient Egyptians. After they found out that one of the red colors was produced by soaking the thread in sheep poop and rotten olive oil and then drying it for six months, they decided to use modern red dye instead.

Religious garments may start as outerwear but move underneath. In the past, Orthodox Jewish men wore the *tallit*—a fringed prayer shawl—around their shoulders all day. Nowadays a smaller fringed shawl, called a *tallit kattan*, is worn under the clothes, and the larger *tallit* is typically worn just for morning prayers.

Some Mormons also place great faith in the protective abilities of their sacred undergarments, which they consider the "armor of God." Consisting of white cotton undershirts and underpants that come down to the knees, "temple garments" are said to shield the wearer from all types of harm. They are worn day and night, throughout life, and many believe that these garments have saved them from fire, bullets, or just the negative influences of society.

WARMTH

"I'm freezing my butt off!" is an expression you've probably heard on a cold day. Though it *is* actually possible to "freeze off" a body part through extreme frostbite (usually toes, fingers, and noses—not butts), we have *lots* of choices when it comes to keeping our bodies warm: moisture-wicking underwear, insulated pants, fleece sweaters, high-tech thermal jackets, even electric socks!

We can get these great cold-weather fashions at the nearest mall, but in earlier times it wasn't that easy. Knowing how to dress for cold weather could be a matter of life or death. And anything you wanted to wear, you had to make yourself! If you lived in a hunting society, you would have to track and kill a deer, then soften, smoke, and dry the skin to make your clothes.

One of the earliest ways discovered for keeping warm was to wear multiple layers of clothing.

Would you like to have lived in a time where you had to tan the hides you would use to make your own clothing?

Different people used different methods of layering, but the idea was the same: to trap warm air between the layers and insulate the body from cold weather. We do the same thing today by putting on T-shirts, sweaters, and jackets in layers.

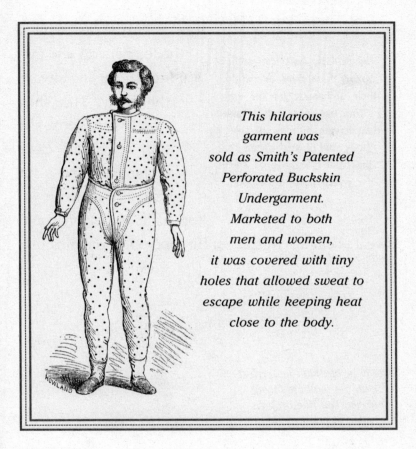

This hilarious garment was sold as Smith's Patented Perforated Buckskin Undergarment. Marketed to both men and women, it was covered with tiny holes that allowed sweat to escape while keeping heat close to the body.

People in really cold climates had a lot of incentive to develop warm underwear. Traditionally, the Inuit people, also called Eskimos, had to lie still on the ice for long periods of time while hunting seals. Not surprisingly, they found some very inventive ways to stay warm. The Inuit created undershirts

Some early American settlers had themselves sewn into their underwear for the winter. This was more comfortable than having buttons all over the body, but it also meant that they didn't bathe until spring rolled around—whew!

out of bird skins, leaving the feathers on and facing them in toward the body. The shirt was worn loose to trap warm air close to the skin, and a fur garment was worn on top of it. A person could sweat heavily in this outfit and still remain dry.

Tweet. Er...ah, tweet...

The Inuit bird-skin undershirt, with the feathers facing in, worked like a down jacket to conserve heat.

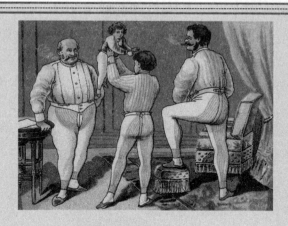

Sometime during the sixteenth century, the word drawers came to be associated with undergarments. A drawer is something that's literally pulled, or "drawn," and comes from the French word tirer (to pull). The "drawers" shown in this picture from the 1800s were developed for sportsmen but found their way to many men's closets as underwear because of their warmth.

The bird skin pulled the moisture away from the body and onto the outside fur. When it hit the cold air, the water froze, and the wearer would just beat it off the outer layer of clothing with a stick.

Many other animal skins have been used throughout history for warmth, including walrus, caribou, goose, and polar bear. Today, many people wear leather, suede, sheepskin, and fur, and they use goose down and other feathers as filling to make warm jackets and blankets. However, these materials are no longer popular for undergarments.

Wool, a natural fiber that comes from sheep, is another material prized for its warmth. Wool can

feel scratchy when worn directly against the skin, but in the days before central heating, people were a lot more willing to put up with a little discomfort in order to keep out the winter chills. There is ample evidence that the undershirts, long underwear, stockings, and petticoats of the last few centuries were made of wool.

Some warm undergarments began as sports equipment and were later embraced by the masses.

Women needed heavy petticoats to keep the cold breezes from blowing up their skirts, because until the nineteenth century, they usually didn't wear any panties underneath!

Long johns, or long knitted underwear, originated with John L. Sullivan, a poor boy from Boston who made a fortune as a bare-knuckled boxer in the late 1800s. Regarded as one of America's first sports superstars, he typically wore long woolen drawers while fighting in cold climates. The design was adapted for use by the average man and nicknamed "long johns."

MODESTY

When a woman of today goes out in a skirt, one of the main reasons she wears underwear is to cover her genitals. If the wind blows her skirt up, or she trips and falls, the worst that can happen is that somebody will get a peek at her panties. This desire to keep certain body parts hidden is called modesty. It has been a major function of undergarments for centuries—although people from different times and places had

There was a time when a young man would have been terribly embarrassed if his peers caught a glimpse of the top of his underwear. But recently it has become fashionable in certain circles for young men to let their pants droop just a bit, allowing the top part of the underwear to be seen.

shockingly different ideas on which areas of the body needed covering.

Those prim and proper women of the American colonies, with their floor-length dresses, usually weren't wearing any underpants! Until the mid-1800s, it was considered scandalously improper for a woman to have *anything* between her legs. That's why women rode sidesaddle (with both legs hanging over the same side of the horse) and why pants were considered a male-only garment. So although a proper lady might have warm stockings that came up to her thighs, and although she might be wearing a thick woolen petticoat under her skirt, the naked truth is that her bottom was bare.

Attitudes about covering the breasts also differ, depending on time and place. In our culture today, we expect women not only to cover their breasts but to wear bras to keep them from jiggling. By contrast, women have gone bare-breasted in many cultures with warm climates.

At various times in history, both men and women have played with the idea of modesty, bending the rules just a bit in order to attract the attention of the opposite sex. For example, a woman of the mid-1800s might have tipped her hoop skirt a few inches to reveal the lacy hem of her petticoat. Or a woman of the early 1900s might have lifted her long dress slightly as she stepped over a puddle, revealing her ankle. It's hard to believe today, but when women were completely covered by layers of clothing, even the glimpse of an ankle seemed very naughty.

In an earlier age, the glimpse of
an ankle was considered sexy.

Folks have sometimes gotten a little carried away by worries about modesty. When X-rays were discovered in 1896, some people became alarmed by the idea that the technology might allow others to see through their clothes. One company took advantage of this fear by making and selling lead-lined underwear, impenetrable to X-rays.

CLEANLINESS

Americans today are accustomed to taking showers every day and putting on clean clothes—particularly underclothes—every morning. Throughout most of history, however, bathing was an infrequent event, and many people

Most modern people would be shocked by the dirt and body odors that were considered perfectly normal in earlier times.

During the time of the American Revolution, a group of fashionable Englishmen nicknamed the "macaronis" promoted the idea of greater personal cleanliness. Due to their influence, it was said that some people began to wash their underwear as often as once a week!

believed it was unhealthy to remove the sweat and body oils that collected on their skin. Clothes were sometimes worn for years without being washed. Leather and suede garments were worn for decades and sometimes even passed down to the next generation. Women's petticoats were worn until they disintegrated.

As fine fabrics and high-quality weaving became widespread, people decided they didn't want their bodily secretions to ruin their expensive and hard-to-launder outer clothing. And so the idea of under-wear as a dirt and odor barrier was born.

The most common undergarment used for this purpose was the smock, which looked something like a nightgown or a long shirt. Both men and women wore variations of the smock for centuries, since it was much easier to wash than an expensive outer garment made of fine fabric. Smocks were usually made of cotton or linen. Wool was avoided because it was more likely to harbor lice—a common affliction among our often filthy ancestors.

A cotton smock.

The smock wasn't totally an undergarment, though. At certain times, it was considered fashionable for women to let bits of lace or ruffles from their smocks peek out from under their dresses. Men sometimes wore the garment like an under-shirt, beneath an outer garment and with the

In the 1800s, women wore corsets made of bone and leather that were never washed. They wore quilted petticoats—which were also never washed—until they disintegrated.

bottom tucked into their pants. Sometimes they wore it alone, the way we wear T-shirts.

In the nineteenth century, wealthy people wanted more than just a cloth barrier between their dirty bodies and their fancy clothes. They wanted to bathe more, a wish that became possible with the advent of innovations like water heaters,

Beau Brummel was considered one of the best-dressed men in London in the early 1800s. A close friend and fashion adviser to Britain's King George IV, he is believed to have introduced the concept of wearing a clean shirt every day. Most people of the early 1800s considered this an absurd, overboard approach to hygiene.

*The "dress protector" and "shirt protector"
were popular undergarments in the days
before the development of antiperspirants.
Their purpose was to absorb underarm sweat
and prevent wet spots from showing on the
outer layer of clothing.
This example from the Dewey Company
of Chicago was worn against bare skin,
but it would have been unthinkable to show that
in an ad, even on a man.*

bathtubs, and indoor plumbing. Once they cleaned up, the wealthy got a little uppity. All of a sudden, the rest of the world was referred to as "the unwashed masses," as the upper classes convinced themselves that cleaner people were actually *better* people. The real difference was that richer people had the money needed to heat water for frequent baths and to employ servants to wash, iron, and starch the many layers of clothing that were now being changed on a regular basis. Have things changed? Ask yourself this: If you were introduced to a dirty, smelly person, would you think badly of him or her?

SUPPORT

One of the most important jobs for underwear is to hold stuff up. That "stuff" can be a body part or another article of clothing. Not surprisingly, people from different historical periods had different ideas about what needed to be held up, held down, or otherwise supported. The most common support garment in the modern world is probably the bra, or brassiere.

A New York woman named Mary Phelps Jacob is credited with fashioning the modern bra. In 1910,

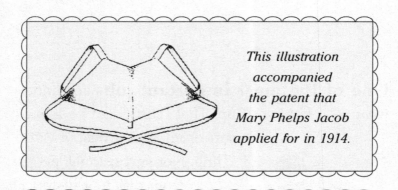

This illustration accompanied the patent that Mary Phelps Jacob applied for in 1914.

Does this look like something your mother uses to strain spaghetti? Well, believe it or not, this is a wire-mesh bra produced in 1885. Its makers claimed that not only would it support a woman's breasts beneath a dress, but the air circulation would allow them to grow better!

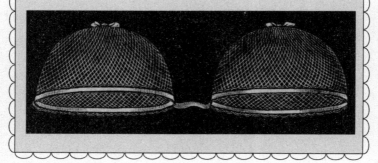

she was getting ready for a party and felt that her breasts needed more support in the dress she had chosen. She had her maid sew together two handkerchiefs with some ribbon and cord—and *voilà!* an invention was born. Mary patented her bra design under the label "brassiere" in 1914 and later sold it to the Warner Brothers Corset Company for a tidy sum.

Though this was the first bra design that became widely available, women have been wrapping material around their chests for centuries. Paintings from the ancient world show female athletes wearing what look like early sports bras. And though it was fashionable in the 1970s for women to go braless, support is now back in style, and many people get downright ornery if they think that a girl or woman looks too "jiggly."

The Case of the Killer Bra: In 1995, a woman named Berbel Zumner was walking through a park in Vienna, Austria, during a storm. The metal in her wire-reinforced bra attracted a bolt of lightning, and she was killed instantly.

This young girl is wearing the Wilson Hose Supporter, which kept her leggings from falling down around her ankles. It was designed for use by both boys and girls and constructed so that it would move along with the body.

Women aren't the only ones who use underwear to reduce the "bounce" factor. Hundreds of products have been invented to keep men's penises and testicles supported during rigorous activity. We call these garments athletic supporters or jockstraps, a name that originated with the "jockey straps" worn by professional riders during those bumpy rides down the racetrack. Men of the 1800s who spent a lot of time on bouncing horse-drawn wagons bought undergarments called suspensories for support.

While male ballet dancers have been accused of padding their underwear to exaggerate their genitals, that's not the case at all. Dancers wear tight, padded jockstraps that are specially designed to hold their genitals flat against the body. Called dance belts, they protect against ligament and abdominal strain during jumps, lifts, and splits.

Today, we tend to think of our bodies as strong and durable, and we condition them through exercise and muscle strengthening. In the late 1800s, however, people seemed to view the body as weak and in constant need of propping up. If you page through

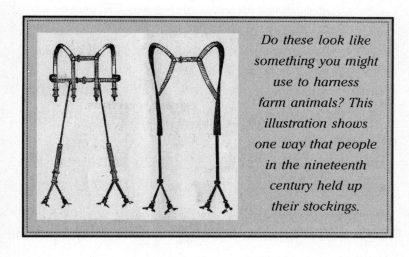

Do these look like something you might use to harness farm animals? This illustration shows one way that people in the nineteenth century held up their stockings.

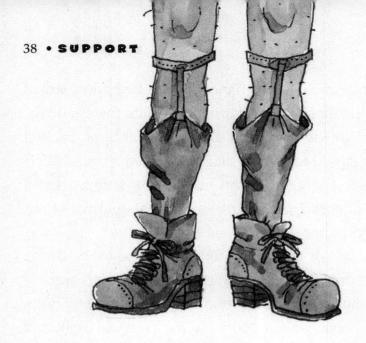

No fashionable gentleman of the 1800s wanted to walk around town with his socks drooping down around his ankles. Sock garters like these kept up his socks and his appearance.

clothing catalogs of that time, you'll see ankle supports, back supports, stomach supports, shoulder supports, and more.

Elastic wasn't invented until 1820, and because it was difficult to produce, many years passed before the product made its way into everyday clothing. Before that time, the question of how to hold up clothing like stockings and petticoats was a real dilemma.

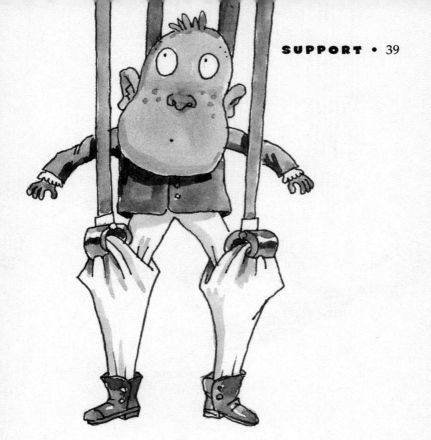

What solution would you invent if the stretch suddenly disappeared from the tops of your socks and underpants?

The garter belt became obsolete in the 1960s when pantyhose took over the market.

Putting on a tight corset was a job for two.
In wealthy households, a maid would do the lacing.

SHAPING

What is the ideal body shape? The answer to that question has changed many times over the centuries. The skinny models and celebrities we see in magazines today would appear unattractive to people in earlier times who admired strong, robust, fleshed-out bodies. A woman with a big, curvy shape is often pressured to diet in today's world, but in other cultures and other times, extra weight was seen as both beautiful and a sign of a family's prosperity.

Clothing, especially underwear, has long been used to change a person's natural shape to fit the fashion of the times. Thin waists, for example, have gone in and out of

What would it be like if you had to wear a corset starting at the age of four? That was the age recommended by corset manufacturers in the late 1800s.

style. Four thousand years ago, the women *and* men of ancient Crete constricted their midsections from childhood onward in order to have hourglass-shaped bodies. The thin-waisted males of Crete were an exception, however. Throughout history, it was usually women who tried every imaginable undergarment to help them attain narrow-waisted silhouettes, often enduring extreme discomfort.

The corset would probably win the prize for the most torturous article of underwear women have had to endure. For hundreds of years, most women in the Western world wore some type of stiff garment around their midsections. At times, the style was to lace the corset so tight that it impaired breathing.

Corsets reached their tightest after 1820, when

Even when corsets were redesigned to lace up the front, they were still difficult to put on. This picture appeared in a corset catalog, demonstrating the best way to get into your corset if you didn't have a servant nearby.

technology allowed corset makers to produce the "lacing holes," or eyelets, from metal. Before then, eyelets had been made of fabric, which tore if the corset was laced too tight.

Corset-making was once an enormous business in the United States. Corsets were considered a must for the properly attired, fashionable woman and were widely marketed. They were produced in large factories providing thousands of jobs. Most early corsets were made of natural fabrics like cotton or linen,

It was thought that certain kinds of "harnesses" helped young ladies learn to have perfect posture at all times. Girls who slumped in their seats were considered to have had a bad upbringing.

which were plentiful and inexpensive. Corsets made for the wealthy were often fancier and constructed from more luxurious materials like silk or satin. So much whalebone was used to stiffen corsets, hoop skirts, and other foolish fashions that the baleen whale was nearly driven to extinction.

Some corsets had a sharp piece of whale baleen (also called whalebone) running through a channel up the front. It was called a "busk," and in an emergency, it could be pulled out and used as a weapon.

Stores carried summer and winter corsets; sports corsets for tennis, horseback riding, and cycling; even children's corsets. One of the most outrageous aspects of corset-wearing in the 1800s was the way mothers forced it upon their daughters at younger and younger ages. Even though they themselves had experienced the pain and restriction of the corset, and even though doctors continually cautioned against it, women felt extreme social pressure to "get their girls in shape" for life as proper ladies and eligible brides.

Scholars have noticed that women seemed to wear corsets during periods in history when their lives were severely restricted and they had few rights in society. As women moved toward equality, they rejected the corset because they wanted to be freer in both mind and body.

Another part of the body that is frequently reshaped is the breast. Amazingly, the ideal way to "wear" one's breasts changes right along with other fashions. Women have hoisted their breasts higher and lower, made them look bigger and smaller, separated them and squished them together, and tried to make them appear more rounded or pointy.

In the late 1700s, devices called bolsters lifted breasts so high that people joked about how hard it was to get a spoonful of soup across the great expanse of cleavage (that's the "valley" between the breasts) without spilling. In the 1920s, fashionable young women wanted a boyish look to go with their newly shortened skirts, so they wore underclothes that flattened their chests. In the 1940s and '50s, so-called "sweater girls" wore pointy bras under tight sweaters.

Does your mother yell at you to "sit up straight"? Consider yourself lucky that you don't live in the late 1800s and early 1900s, when proper posture was considered far more important than it is today. Young girls were strapped into shoulder harnesses that forced them to sit upright and behave in a lady-like manner.

Men in positions of authority, such as army officers and society gentlemen, often wore back supporters, girdles, and other undergarments that forced them to stand board-straight. They felt that this made them look more confident and in charge. During the Civil War, one Confederate general credited his military posture with saving his life. Riding his horse in battle, General John Brown Gordon felt a bullet whiz across his back, tearing through his coat but missing the spine. He made a point of telling his men that slouching would have cost him his life.

Some women stuffed their bustles with bran, which was said to attract the appetites of nearby farm animals.

EXAGGERATION

Underwear has frequently been used to exaggerate the size of body parts. What parts? Well, whatever parts were considered especially attractive at that time in history. (And it's not always the parts you might think!)

For example, in the late 1700s, European men wore long pants that were very tight around the lower leg. This highlighted the calf muscles—in those days considered an especially attractive feature by the ladies. Of course, men with good-looking leg muscles thought tight pants were just fine and dandy, but skinny-legged guys were left feeling thoroughly inadequate. To address this problem, the "artificial calf," or calf pad, was invented. Strapped to the back of the legs and hidden beneath the pants, calf pads gave the illusion of well-toned legs.

The bottom is another area that the fashion-conscious have been prone to exaggerate. Bustles, worn underneath dresses to keep the back of the skirt from dragging, became a popular way to emphasize

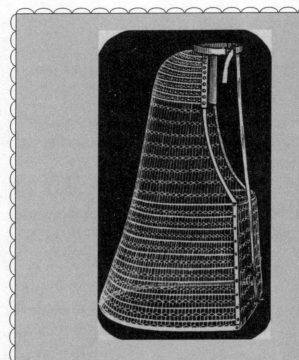

This metal cage is one of the more extreme bustle styles of the late 1800s. Are you wondering how the woman who wore this sat down? She didn't! She had to be willing to stand all evening in order to look fashionable.

this part of women's bodies. They were made from many different materials and took many different shapes over time, but the general idea was to wear something around the waist that created a "pouf" on the posterior.

Some women wore bustles stuffed with cork. Others used deer hair, horsehair, wire mesh, wool, or cotton. Even bran, the husks of cereal grain left over when flour is ground, was used to achieve a ballooning backside. Today we use bran to fill pincushions, and if you've ever squeezed one, you know what a stuffed bustle felt like. Bran had its drawbacks, however: there were reports of farm animals attempting to munch on the backsides of nearby women wearing bustles stuffed with this material.

A truly ingenious bustle was designed to address a simple problem. Women wanted to sit down! Developed by Stapley and Smith of London, it folded up and out of the way for sitting. When the wearer stood up, springs would cause it to pop back into position.

Falsie is a slang word for any device stuffed into the bra to make the breasts look bigger. Falsies reached the height of their popularity in the 1950s, when big, pointy breasts were all the rage. In 1955, researchers in Britain estimated that three out of every four women in the country were using some kind of falsie, or "cutie," as they were called there.

Because most falsies were simply tucked inside the bra, they were known to slip out at the most inconvenient times. Almost every girl who was a teenager during the 1950s knows somebody whose falsie popped out of her evening gown or escaped from her bathing suit and floated across the pool.

Women who couldn't get the look or feel they wanted with falsies or padded bras sometimes turned

This early inflatable bra from the Mrs. Fletcher Company
promised a "perfectly faultless bosom formation."
The little sticklike objects are straws used for inflation.

to air for promised better results: since at least the 1950s, manufacturers have experimented with inflatable bras that wearers could blow up like balloons!

The weirdest piece of clothing used for exaggeration was probably the codpiece, which started out as a simple, modest undergarment and turned into a padded, jeweled monstrosity that made men's genitals appear bigger.

The story of the codpiece begins hundreds of years

ago when men's "breeches," or pants, were nothing more than two separate legs tied to a belt. It didn't really matter that the breeches left men's bottoms uncovered, because they wore long shirtlike tunics over them. However, in the fourteenth century, shorter tunics came into style. As the hemlines rose higher and higher, men found it hard to swing their legs up onto their horses without putting on a show for onlookers. To maintain modesty, a simple pouch was added to the space between the two pants legs. But there was an unexpected benefit: men found that not only did the codpiece provide coverage, it was also a nifty storage compartment! Coins, handkerchiefs, and other small items that used to be carried in leather bags hanging from the waist (where they were often stolen by "cutpurse" thieves) could now be safely hidden in the codpiece.

Over time, the codpiece evolved from a practical piece of clothing to an item that was purely for show, especially when worn by noblemen. By the time King Henry VIII came along, the codpiece was padded to enormous proportions and even decorated with jewels! (There is a famous portrait of this king that shows him with an obvious bulge sticking out from beneath his robes.) Luckily for the men of today, the codpiece faded from use by the end of the sixteenth century.

Codpieces appear in thousands of formal portraits from the fifteenth, sixteenth, and seventeenth centuries. Yet many historians in the years since have found the codpiece so embarrassing that they routinely left it out of fashion history books. At times, portraits were redrawn so the codpiece could be removed.

*These drawings contrast the clothing of a wealthy woman
of the late 1800s with the clothing of a maid. The wealthy
woman wears a wide, ruffle-covered dress that would barely fit
through a doorway. Depending on the type of undergarments worn
beneath the dress, she may not have been able to sit down easily.*

STATUS

Your "status" is how important you appear in the eyes of your community. As unfair as it may be, a rich person is typically granted more status than a poor person, and someone from a "distinguished" family is often viewed as more important than an ordinary Joe. Clothes, even underclothes, have been used for centuries as a way to display wealth and status.

The working woman wears a slightly flared skirt in an attempt to keep up with fashion, but she has to be practical if she wants to do her job. The bending, lifting, and cleaning that make up her day would be impossible in the rich woman's clothes.

Sometimes a person shows wealth by wearing up-to-date styles or expensive fabrics. There have also been several periods in history when women displayed their wealth by wearing awkward fashions that prevented them from doing just about anything useful. In the late nineteenth century, upper-class women wore enormous undergarments or layers of petticoats to make their skirts stand out from the body. It was a very obvious way of proclaiming their families'

Even simple activities like walking through doors or gates became major undertakings when wearing wide petticoats.

status, since only the wealthy could afford to simply sit around and look fashionable all day.

Before petticoats were invented, the only way women could get their skirts to flare outward below the waist was by pleating (folding) the material. But around 1500, some adventurous trendsetter found that circles of willow branches could be used to make skirts even bigger. At first, dressmakers sewed these wooden hoops into each dress, but then they decided it would be easier to create a special undergarment that could be worn with any dress in the closet. This was the farthingale, which influenced the shape of women's clothing for over two hundred years.

Wearing a farthingale made a skirt stick out all the way around: front, sides, and back. But over time, it became more fashionable to have the skirt jut out only on the sides, as if a woman were carrying two baskets beneath her dress, one on each hip. The undergarment used to get this shape was called a pannier, which means "basket" in French.

Pannier frames were made of plant material or

The popular writer Fanny Fern once remarked that women ought to be paid by the city of New York for sweeping its streets with their petticoats every time they took a walk.

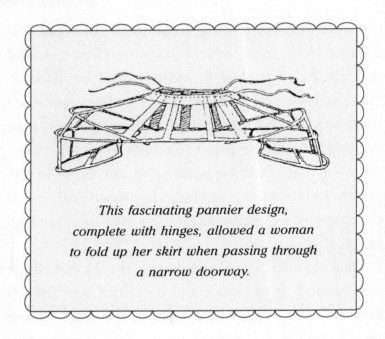

This fascinating pannier design,
complete with hinges, allowed a woman
to fold up her skirt when passing through
a narrow doorway.

whalebone and covered with cloth. They started out small, but like so many other fashions, the pannier became more and more extreme. When the style

became too big to fit through doorways, a bit of engineering was applied to the design. Soon the most fashionable ladies were wearing hinged panniers that folded out of the way when necessary and enabled the skirt to be lifted off the ground with handles. At

Women used to starch their petticoats to achieve greater skirt volume. But that also meant they had to be extra careful around fireplaces, because starch is flammable.

the height of the pannier craze, in the mid- to late 1770s, some royal ladies wore skirts measuring up to six feet across.

In the mid-1800s, enormous skirts enjoyed another period of popularity among the wealthy. Women wore multiple petticoats, starching them for greater volume. The petticoats were also stiffened with horsehair, or "crin," which was the reason these garments were called crinoline petticoats. These heavy layers of petticoats required a great deal of time to wash, iron, and starch.

Because petticoats were often hooked to the corset, the corset had to be laced even tighter to keep the heavy outfit from ending up in a heap around the ankles. Multiple petticoats were also somewhat unsanitary, sweeping up dirt, bugs, and bacteria and carrying them back into the home. And since starch is flammable, a woman had to be extremely cautious near fireplaces.

These absurdly cumbersome fashions angered those who were working hard for women's rights. Though many of these activists came from wealthy families, they did not see the oversize fashions of the day as symbols of their status. To them, restrictive clothing was just one more thing that held women back from being equal participants in society.

In 1851 a few brave souls, led by Amelia Bloomer, began wearing a new style of clothing that featured a shorter skirt with pants underneath. Nicknamed "bloomers" by the press, the outfit and its wearers

Contrary to popular opinion, Amelia Bloomer didn't design the garment that carried her name. She did, however, capture the attention of the press by bravely demonstrating it in public. This paved the way for more practical women's clothing for sports. This Smith College basketball team of 1902 wore bloomers.

Truth or fiction?
Legend has it that in 1862, a woman attempting suicide by jumping from a bridge in Bristol, England, was saved by her cage crinoline, which acted almost like a parachute to slow her descent.

were mercilessly mocked whenever they appeared in public. Many people were greatly disturbed by the fact that women, by wearing pants, seemed to be intruding on male territory. Bloomers were denounced as "improper" and "foreign," and were harshly criticized in newspaper cartoons. Few women wanted to endure this degree of public humiliation, and bloomers quickly disappeared from the fashion landscape. However, the practical aspects of the outfit were hard to ignore, and bloomers paved the way for women to begin wearing pants for cycling, horseback riding, and other sports. Women (and their aching backs) got a bit of relief in 1856 with the invention of the "cage crinoline," an undergarment made of graduated hoops of cane, whalebone, or steel. A fashionable lady could discard her heavy petticoats but still achieve the same bell-shaped look with one easier-to-wear garment. Women were thrilled by the lightweight, springy feeling of the new wood or wire device and the way it allowed air to circulate around their legs in summer. Another advantage of the cage was that it cut down on the amount of laundry you had to do (or, in the cases of most of the women wearing these items, the amount of laundry your maid had to do).

Women rushed to buy cage crinolines, which freed them from the weight of many petticoats. They became so popular that an estimated 3,000 tons of steel a year were needed to manufacture them in the United States. Even Amelia Bloomer gave up her outfit when the cage crinoline became available.

Yet cage crinolines had some serious drawbacks. They were hard to control on windy days and sometimes blew inside out like umbrellas in a tornado. And they tipped up in the back every time the woman leaned forward. (Not surprisingly, both these problems led to the increased wearing of underpants.) And if you took too big a step forward, your foot could catch on the bottom hoop and you'd tumble over. Like petticoats, crinolines could also catch on fire if the wearer brushed too close to the

Humorists had a great time poking fun at how the cage crinoline became unruly on windy days.

fireplace. Women were cautioned that the cage-like shape could act like a chimney, causing a quick and deadly blaze.

Today, just as in the past, clothing can display a person's wealth or poverty, reveal his or her status. Think about an executive woman with manicured nails, high heels, and a tailored skirt. Would she ever be mistaken for the office cleaner who must wear practical, washable garments and flat shoes to do her job?

MAKING A STATEMENT

*I*n the last century especially, many people have used underwear to get the attention of the public, whether for personal or political reasons. In the 1960s, "bra burners" protested the way society discriminated against women and imposed restrictive rules governing their appearance.

During World War II, when the Marines wanted to show that they were treating film star Tyrone Power just like any other soldier, they released a picture of him hanging his own underwear out to dry.

They probably should have been called "bra trashers" instead of "bra burners," because the original group simply threw bras, girdles, wigs, cosmetics, and other "beauty" items into a trash can while cameras rolled outside the 1968 Miss America Pageant. While the public typically viewed such stunts as silly, they served to get people talking about equality for women.

Exposing someone's underwear is a long-standing technique for causing shame and embarrassment. For example, after the Nazis were driven out of France near the end of World War II, the public took out their anger on those who had collaborated with the enemy. French women who had relationships with German soldiers were publicly humiliated, not only by having their heads shaved but by being forced to walk through the streets in their underwear.

In 1969, women decided to publicly toss their bras into the Chicago River in support of women's liberation. They were fined for littering. And it made for some strange catches downstream!

Even *speaking* about someone's underwear can be a way of insulting them. In 1980, an education official named John Phillips wanted to question the abilities of the new U.S. Department of Education, so he publicly stated his worry that the agency might be "just another federal bureaucracy run by a group of people with their feet caught in their underwear." And the phrase "Don't get your panties in a knot" (or the British "Don't get your knickers in a twist") is a way of saying, "I think you're wrong to get so worked up about this, so calm down." Another example: Back in 1896, when William Allen White, editor of the *Emporia Gazette* of Kansas, wanted to insult a politician he considered out-of-date, he referred to him as an "old human hoop skirt."

Underwear can also be used to convey respect. In the Victorian period, people who lost loved ones were expected to follow very strict rules of mourning. A widow wore black mourning clothes of varying degrees for more than two years. Under the mourning dresses, a woman would wear either a black petticoat or a white petticoat with a black ribbon sewn around the bottom. It would have been disrespectful to allow the white of the petticoat to be seen below the black dress.

Underwear has also been used to make rebellious fashion statements. In the 1780s, Marie Antoinette, the famed French queen who was later beheaded, shocked France by wearing chemise dresses at court. Up to that time, the chemise (which looked like a long nightgown) was worn only as an undergarment.

Marlon Brando helped to turn men's cotton undershirts into outerwear (now called T-shirts) in the 1951 film *A Streetcar Named Desire*. Madonna did the same for the bustier (a long-line bra) in the 1980s film *Desperately Seeking Susan*. Singer David Bowie appeared onstage with a jockstrap outside his clothing in the 1970s. (Happily, this did not spark a fashion trend.)

College boys of the 1950s thought it was fun to storm the girls' dorms and steal their underwear, which they would then publicly display. These immature outings were called "panty raids."

For some reason, there are many stories about female patriots giving up their undergarments in time of war, or using their undergarments to somehow assist their side in the conflict. In the DAR (Daughters of the American Revolution) Museum in Washington, D.C., sits a charming silver bell shaped like a petticoat. It was designed to commemorate the story of Anna Warner Bailey, who donated her flannel petticoats to be used for gun wadding during the War of 1812.

During the Civil War, a southern woman named Belle Edmondson is said to have smuggled supplies to Confederate soldiers under her skirts. Other women traveled with hidden messages. The government asked women to stop buying corsets during World War I, reportedly freeing up thousands of tons of steel that were diverted to shipbuilding.

And during World War II, women donated their nylon stockings to be made into parachutes.

FUTURE UNDIES

What will the future hold in the wonderful world of underwear? The story is always being rewritten, as clothing changes to satisfy different people in different times. A Japanese firm has experimented with making undergarments out of recycled plastic. A British woman has developed a bra that monitors the heartbeat and sounds an alarm if the wearer is threatened. And the Russians are developing bacteria to eat the dirty underwear of astronauts on long space missions. What can we say, except Long Live Underwear!

You've seen pictures of American astronauts in their bulky spacesuits, but did you ever wonder what they wear underneath? One of the layers is long underwear with water tubes running through it. Cool liquid circulates through the tubes, keeping the astronaut comfortable during periods of strenuous activity. Because a typical spacesuit has so many layers, and because of the pure oxygen pumped into it, the body cannot cool down without assistance.

In the 1994 movie *Blankman*, the main character is a superhero who invents bulletproof underwear, which he wears in his crime fighting.

Fans of the legendary Russian ballet dancer Nijinsky stole his underwear from his dressing room while he was performing. Similarly, fans of crooner Frank Sinatra stole his underwear off the wash line of his mother's house in Hoboken, NJ.

Though they were worn completely out of sight beneath dresses, bustles were often covered with decorative ribbons and lace.

Julia Archibald Holmes, credited as being the first woman to climb Pike's Peak, made the trek in 1858 in bloomers.

In 1998 in Gloucester, England, a man named Alan Myatt played the part of Henry VIII in the "Merrie Englande" summer festival. When he needed to be on-call for his job, he simply tucked his cell phone into the costume's codpiece for safekeeping.

The Southern Traverse is a famous endurance race in New Zealand. In 1997 a team from Brazil became stranded. While awaiting assistance, they burned their underwear for warmth.

Police were called to an Ohio restroom where a woman had suffered a gunshot wound. She told the officers she had been keeping a gun hidden in her underpants. When she pulled them down to use the toilet, the gun fell out, hit the floor, and fired, shooting her in the leg.

Underwear is a favorite place for criminals to hide stolen or illegal items, in hopes that police will not search there. A Frenchman was once caught trying to smuggle an endangered boa constrictor out of Colombia in his underpants. Police in Cincinnati arrested a woman for possession of marijuana, which was hidden in her bra. A man arrested in Wisconsin for hiding cocaine in his underpants tried to convince police that the underpants were not his!

As late as the 1920s, books on household management recommended washing underwear only twice a week.

In 1994, a pair of the late Elvis Presley's underpants were stolen from the Ripley's Believe It or Not! Museum in Los Angeles. The underpants were custom-designed with special elastic so Elvis would remain comfortable during his on-stage gyrations.

Scent-Lok is the brand name of an underwear line developed for bow hunters. A layer of charcoal in the garments absorbs body odor, preventing animals from picking up the hunter's scent.

Scouts have been singing versions of the song
"God Bless My Underwear"
around the campfire for years.
(Sung to the tune of "God Bless America")

God bless my underwear,
All fourteen pairs.
Stand inside them,
And guide them,
Through the holes,
Through the rips,
Through the tears.
From the washer,
To the dryer,
To the dresser,
To derrieres,
God bless my underwear,
All fourteen pairs.
God bless my underwear,
All fourteen pairs.

THE END

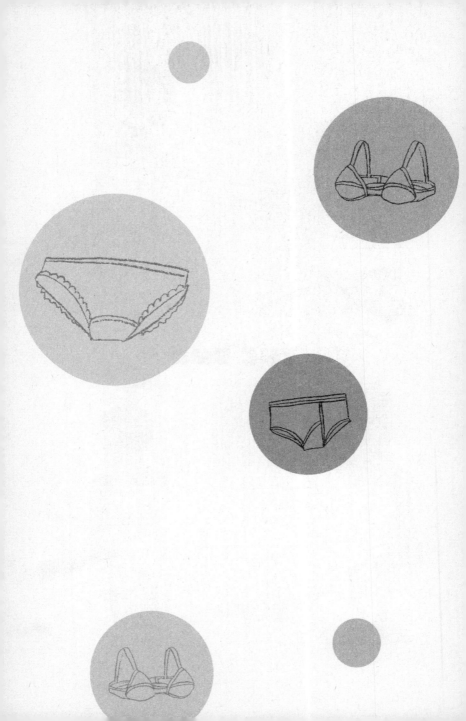